BIODIVERSITY

By Carla Mooney

ROurke
Educational Media
rourkeeducationalmedia.com

Teacher Notes available at
rem4teachers.com

www.rourkeeducationalmedia.com

PHOTO CREDITS: Cover and title page © Vladimir Melnikov, WillSelarep, abxyz, Simon Hack, Martin Strmko, wsfurlan, Shoemcfly, Jan Rysavy, David Yang, Nick Biemans, Henrick Jonsson, Sergey Yakovlev; Pages 2/3 © Rich Carey; Pages 4/5 © Ralph Loesche, Eduardo Rivero, Vladimir Melnik, Brandon Alms, scaners3d; Pages 6/7 © Vaclav Volrab, Zuzule, Waranon, Lenkadan, Photosani, vseb; Pages 8/9 © Rich Carey, Evgeny Kovalev spb, Dima_Rogozhin, Inga Nielsen; Pages 10/11 © Yuriy Kulyk, Dudarev Mikhail, Kjersti Joergensen, Pavlo Loushkin, Brians, Dominik Michalek; Pages 12/13 © Sten Porse, Lee319, javarman, orxy, Andrew McDonough, nodff; Pages 14/15 © Wilm Ihlenfeld, pixelpics, Jean-Edouard Rozey; Pages 16/17 © Jakub Pavlinec, Paul Aniszewski, imagestalk, rck_953, Steve Byland, Volha Ahranovich, Titanchik, Jakub Pavlinec, yuris, GRASS, chantal de bruijne, Kokhanchikov, Fedorov Oleksiy; Pages 18/19 © Konstantin Mironov, CCat82, Cyrillic; Pages 20/21 © Jose Antonio Perez, XAOC, Nikolaj Kondratenko, Pecold, Rechitan Sorin; Pages 22/23 © Goluba, ra3rn; Pages 24/25 © Alessio Marrucci, Dr. Morley Read; Pages 26/27 © InavanHateren, Houshmand Rabbani, idiz, Brendan Howard; Pages 28/29 © Demid Borodin, Poznyakov, ehtesham, Jim Agronick; Pages 30/31 © Olaf Speier, Rich Carey, tubuceo; Pages 32/33 © Goodluz, Krzysztof Odziomek; Pages 34/35 © NOAA, Bonita R. Cheshier; Pages 36/37 © USDA, Stuart-Fox D, Moussalli A; Pages 38/39 © Iakov Filimonov, USFWS; Pages 40/41 © SNEHIT, Julie Lubick, Frontpage, Antoni Murcia, mary416, Dray van Beeck, Nastya Pirieva, Jim Agronick; Pages 42/43 © Ninjatacoshell, Radoslaw Lecyk; Pages 44/45 © Joy Fera, J.D.S., Jill Chen

Edited by Precious McKenzie
Cover design by Teri Intzegian
Interior design Blue Door Publishing, FL

Library of Congress PCN Data

Biodiversity / Carla Mooney
(Let's Explore Science)
ISBN 978-1-61810-127-3 (hard cover) (alk. paper)
ISBN 978-1-61810-260-7 (soft cover)
Library of Congress Control Number: 2011945272

Rourke Educational Media
Printed in the United States of America,
North Mankato, Minnesota

rourkeeducationalmedia.com

customerservice@rourkeeducationalmedia.com • PO Box 643328 Vero Beach, Florida 32964

Table of Contents

Ch 1   What is Biodiversity? 4

Ch 2   Biodiversity in Earth's Biomes 10

Ch 3   Web of Life 16

Ch 4   Importance of Biodiversity 18

Ch 5   Threats to Biodiversity 24

Ch 6   Studying Biodiversity 32

Ch 7   Protecting Biodiversity 38

        Glossary 46

        Index 48

CHAPTER ONE

What is Biodiversity?

Did you know that scientists have identified more than 1.7 million **species** living on Earth? There are insects, plants, fish, reptiles, amphibians, birds, and mammals living on the land, in the air, and in the water. And those are just the ones you can see! There are also millions of **microorganisms** that live all around us that you can't see.

toucan

bromeliad

Rainforests hold some of the richest and most diverse ecosystems in the world. More than half of the world's plant and animal species live in rainforests.

That's not all. Scientists believe that there are millions more living on Earth that have not been discovered yet. That's a lot of living things!

Biodiversity is a simple idea. It is the enormous variety of life on Earth. It includes all of the plants, animals, fungi, and other living things in an area. This life is interconnected, like pieces of a puzzle.

red-eyed tree frog

sundew plant

An easy way to measure biodiversity is to count the number of species in an area. Scientists **classify** similar living things in groups called species. For example, horses, ladybugs, and roses are all different species. Areas with a large number of different species have high biodiversity.

quarter horses

While quarter horses, ladybugs, and water lilies may live and grow in the same area, each belongs to a different species.

ladybugs

water lilies

Another type of biodiversity is in an organism's genes. The cells of all living **organisms** have genes. Genes hold the instructions that decide what the organism looks like and how it works. Every species has different genes. That is what makes a tree different from a horse.

poodle

retriever

boxer

Biodiversity can also be the variety of **ecosystems** where organisms live. An ecosystem is a community of living things and their physical environment. Coral reefs, wetlands, deserts, and forests are examples of ecosystems. The animals, plants, and other living things on Earth live in different ecosystems.

Name The Ecosystem!

What kinds of animals live here?

wetland

forest

desert

Each place has its own characteristics and **climate**. Is it hot or cold? Is it wet or dry? The climate of each ecosystem affects its biodiversity. Together, the variety of species, genes, and ecosystems make up Earth's biodiversity.

Did You Know?

The largest living organism on Earth is a coral reef called The Great Barrier Reef off Australia.

9

CHAPTER TWO

Biodiversity in Earth's Biomes

Biodiversity is affected by the climate and characteristics of an area. Areas that are warm year round generally have the highest biodiversity. More living things make their homes in these places. Areas with warm summers and cold winters generally have less biodiversity. Colder areas like mountaintops usually have even less biodiversity.

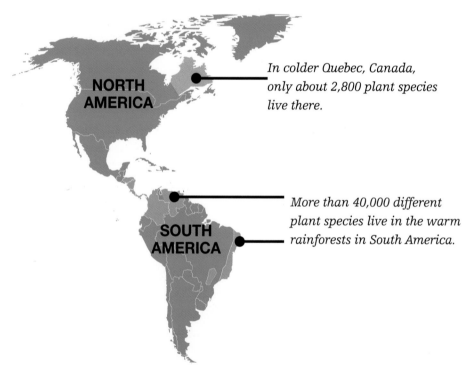

NORTH AMERICA

In colder Quebec, Canada, only about 2,800 plant species live there.

SOUTH AMERICA

More than 40,000 different plant species live in the warm rainforests in South America.

Scientists have classified areas of Earth as **biomes**. A biome is a specific area that has a similar climate. A biome is like a very large ecosystem. Within a biome, the animals and plants depend on each other to live. Scientists have named six major types of biomes.

Freshwater Biome

The freshwater biome includes freshwater bodies of water such as ponds, lakes, streams, rivers, and wetlands. These bodies of water are low in salt, usually less than 1 percent.

Marine Biome

The marine biome includes oceans, coral reefs, and estuaries. These biomes cover about three-fourths of the Earth's surface.

Desert Biome

On land, dry desert biomes cover about one-fifth of the Earth's surface. In deserts, it rains less than 20 inches (50 centimeters) per year.

Forest Biome

The forest biome covers over two-thirds of the Earth's land. It has trees and other woody vegetation.

Grassland Biome

The grassland biome is covered with grasses instead of large shrubs or trees.

Tundra Biome

The tundra is the coldest biome. It usually has very cold temperatures and little rain or snow. The North Pole is part of the tundra biome.

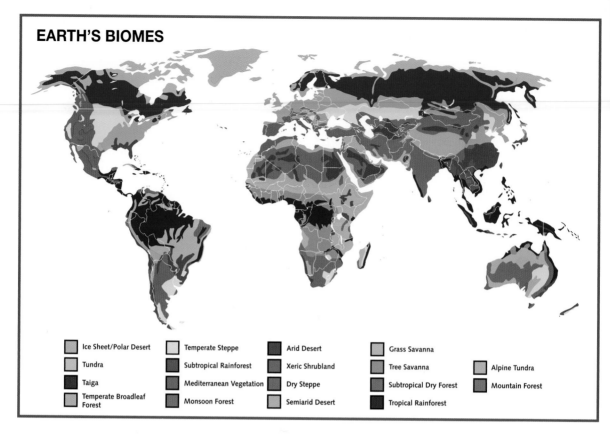

EARTH'S BIOMES

Ice Sheet/Polar Desert	Temperate Steppe	Arid Desert	Grass Savanna
Tundra	Subtropical Rainforest	Xeric Shrubland	Tree Savanna	Alpine Tundra
Taiga	Mediterranean Vegetation	Dry Steppe	Subtropical Dry Forest	Mountain Forest
Temperate Broadleaf Forest	Monsoon Forest	Semiarid Desert	Tropical Rainforest

Life in each of the world's biomes is very different. As a result, animals, plants, and other living things have **adapted** to live in each place. The adaptation may be a body part, covering, or behavior that helps an animal survive.

Many animals have body parts that help them live in their environment. Macaws use their large beaks to crack open large nuts and grab the fruit inside.

macaw

Blue-footed boobies have streamlined beaks and heads to help them dive deeper into water to catch fish.

A giraffe's neck is an adaptation that helps it reach leaves.

Body coverings can protect an animal from its environment. Many mammals have hair or fur to keep them warm in colder climates. Birds have feathers to keep them warm in winter and help them fly. Amphibians have moist, slick skin that is good for the water.

Thick fur keeps a bison warm during winter months.

Skin coloring helps some amphibians blend into their surroundings.

Some types of body coverings **camouflage** or hide animals from predators or prey. Striped fur helps an animal blend into its environment. A tiger's stripes help it match nearby plants. This makes it almost invisible to other animals. Other types of body covering adaptations include brightly covered feathers, spotted fur, and scales. Each covering helps the animal in its specific environment.

The pattern of this butterfly's wings allows it to blend into its background.

Did You Know?

Adaptations can also affect an animal's actions. Animals in Africa migrate at specific times of the year to find water. Migration is a learned behavior that has helped animals survive.

Every year, herds of African wildebeest migrate more than 350 miles (563 km) from Tanzania to Kenya and back again in search of food and water.

Adaptations happen over a long period of time. They usually happen when a gene changes by accident. Some accidental changes help the animal or plant survive better than others do. These survivors pass on the changed gene to their young. This change in a species over a long period of time is called evolution.

Monarch butterflies are not able to survive the cold winters of most of the United States so they migrate south and west each fall to escape the cold weather.

15

CHAPTER THREE

Web of Life

Within each biome, life is connected like the strands on a web. From the tiniest algae to the largest mammal, all species depend on each other. Forests provide shelter for animals and plants. Fungi eat dead material and release nutrients into the soil. Plants use the nutrients to grow. Insects and animals eat plants. Insects also carry pollen from one plant to another, allowing the plant to reproduce. Larger animals eat smaller animals and insects.

High biodiversity is a sign of a healthy biome. When there is less biodiversity, the connected links between living things may break. All the species in the biome may be harmed.

Forest Food Web

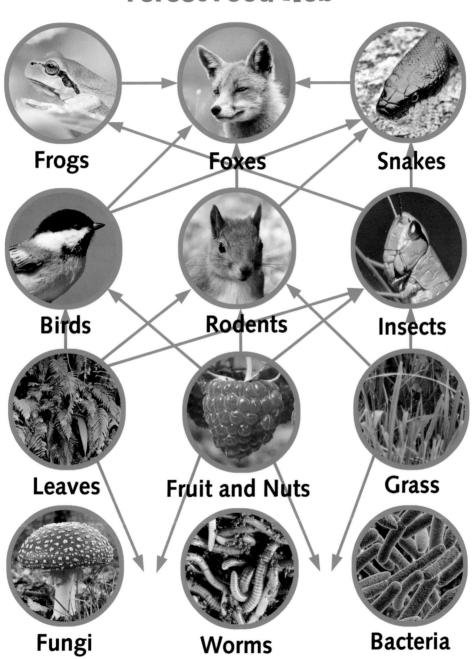

CHAPTER FOUR

Importance of Biodiversity

A diverse ecosystem helps to keep nature in balance and our planet livable. Ecosystems with high biodiversity are usually stronger. For example, a forest with many tree species will be better able to survive if one tree species dies because of epidemic disease. Ecosystems with high biodiversity are also better able to recover from a natural disaster like a flood or tornado.

Some ecosystems rely on naturally occurring fires to regulate growth. Still, too much fire can upset natural ecosystem cycles, destroy native plants, and encourage the growth of fire-dependent species like the Bishop Pine.

Did You Know?

Some tree species are fire dependent, like the Bishop Pine. This ability ensures that the Bishop Pine trees will survive, and in fact thrive, if a fire starts.

Forest Flood!

Which species have been damaged?
How do you think this area
will recover?

Biodiversity is important to people for many reasons. Plants release oxygen into the air, which helps us breathe. Leafy plants cool us with shade they provide and the moisture they release. In wetlands, plants, animals, and microorganisms act as sponges. They filter out sediment and waste from entering rivers, oceans, and lakes. This keeps our drinking water, lakes, and rivers clean. If biodiversity declines, these natural processes may not work as well.

Wetland plants work to keep the Earth's water clean. They act as a natural filter to prevent sediment, pollution, and other impurities from reaching rivers, lakes, and oceans.

Biodiversity is important to many industries. People who work in industries such as agriculture, food supply and restaurants, construction, medicine, and tourism rely on biodiversity. Healthy ecosystems provide a variety of food, like meat and plants that people eat.

We build our houses, toys, and other products with wood from nature.

People visit lakes, rivers, and oceans for swimming and other water sports. They climb mountains and ski down snowy slopes. Others spend time exploring forest trails in community parks. When biodiversity decreases, these activities may suffer.

Biodiversity is also an important part of medicine and health research. Scientists have discovered that some chemicals in plants and other living things can be used in medicines.

The bark from the Pacific yew tree is used to treat certain types of cancer.

Medicine made from salmon is used during heart surgery.

To date, scientists have only studied a small number of species that could be used in medicines. As biodiversity drops, a plant or other organism that could make a life-saving medicine may be lost forever.

Microorganisms were the starting points for antibiotics like penicillin.

Did You Know?

About 25 percent of the medicines used today are taken from or based on chemicals found in plants, animals, or other living things.

CHAPTER FIVE

Threats to Biodiversity

Over the past 100 years, biodiversity has decreased significantly. Many plants and animals have become **extinct**. Sometimes extinction is a natural process. A species dies out while a new species develops to take its place. Scientists say that plant and animal species are becoming extinct at 1,000 times the natural rate. Many believe that the actions of humans have changed the natural process of extinction.

The loss of biodiversity around the world has many causes. This causes the number of healthy places for animals and plants to live to shrink. Today, plants and animals face many threats, including **habitat loss**, **introduced species**, climate change, and pollution.

Baiji River Dolphin

This dolphin used to live in the Yangtze River in China. In 2006, it was classified as extinct.

Golden Toad

Amphibians are disappearing quickly from Costa Rica. This toad went extinct in 1992.

Tasmanian Tiger

Settlers in Tasmania hunte this species to extinction. Experts believe it went extinct in the 1930s.

At this rate, Earth faces the greatest extinction crisis since the dinosaurs became extinct 65 million years ago.

The world's human population is growing. As the human population grows, people need more places to live and work. People clear land to build homes, cities, and roads. They remove native plants from land to create farmland. They cut down trees to use as building lumber. The plants, shrubs, and trees in these habitats provided food and shelter for many species. When large areas of land are cleared, fewer animals and plants can live in the remaining habitat.

Slash-and-burn is used to clear some rainforests for farming land. The rainforest is cut down and the vegetation is left to die. Anything left is burned and the land is turned into farmland. At first, the fire's ashes provide nutrients to the soil for farm corps. After a few years, the soil becomes nutrient-depleted and too poor to grow crops.

Did You Know?

Rainforests are some of the most biodiverse places on Earth. About half of all known plant and animal species live in rainforests. Land clearing in rainforests is a serious threat to biodiversity. Many species cannot survive after their homes are destroyed. Scientists say that at the current rate of land clearing, the world's rainforests could disappear within 100 years.

Introduced Species

Introduced species are plants and animals brought from their natural habitat to live in a new habitat. People have intentionally brought plants and animals to new areas for farming, hunting, or as pets. Other times, species such as mice, rats, insects, and fungi have accidentally traveled to a new habitat. Some examples of introduced species are rabbits in Australia and the European starling in North America.

If an introduced species survives, it can become a serious threat to biodiversity. The introduced species competes with native plants and animals for food and nutrients. Introduced plants may crowd out sunlight and nutrients from other plants. They may overgrow and prevent other plants from growing.

Purple loosestrife is an invasive species that displaces native wetland vegetation. The invasion often begins with a few plants that eventually spread rapidly and take over an entire wetland. The plant can overrun thousands of acres of wetlands, causing some native plant species to disappear.

Introduced animals eat the food and take shelter used by native animals. They may eat the eggs or young of native animals. It may also bring disease to the new habitat. If the introduced species reproduces in large numbers, it can become a pest.

AUSTRALIA

Sydney

Melbourne

on rabbit

wallaby

Rabbits in Australia compete with native wallabies for food in their new habitat. They also cause millions of dollars of damage to Australian crops each year.

Overconsumption of Resources

The rising number of people using natural resources threatens biodiversity. **Overconsumption** happens when people use animals or plants faster than they can reproduce naturally. Ocean habitats are especially at risk from over consumption. Many fish that we eat, such as herring, cod, sardines, and tuna, have decreased in the wild because of overfishing. As fish species are lost, it affects the entire ocean ecosystem.

Shark Hunting

Millions of sharks are killed each year from overfishing. Many are accidentally caught in fishing nets. Others are killed for their meat or fins. Sharks are an important part of the ocean's food webs. Fewer sharks in the water could upset the balance of the food web and affect other ocean species.

Fish   Sea Lions   Sharks

Small fish are eaten by sea lions, who in turn become prey for the great white shark.

Every year, more than 170 billion pounds of wild fish and shellfish are caught in the oceans.

Pollution

Bug spray, lawn fertilizers, and other chemicals make our lives easier. They are also a threat to biodiversity. When toxic chemicals from industry, farming, or neighborhoods leak into the environment, they can kill or damage plants and animals.

At Risk For Extinction!

Many species around the world are at risk for extinction.

1 in 4 mammals

1 in 8 birds

1 in 3 amphibians

1 in 5 plants

1 in 3 corals

Climate Change

Throughout history, the Earth's climate has slowly changed. Over time, ecosystems and species adapt to new conditions or new species develop. When climate changes rapidly, plants and animals are less able to adapt.

Today, warmer ocean temperatures threaten the world's coral reefs. Coral reefs are some of the most biodiverse places on Earth. A single reef can be home to more than 3,000 fish species and other sea creatures. Since the nineteenth century, global ocean temperatures have risen by 1.3 degrees Fahrenheit (0.74 degrees Celsius). When water temperature rises, the algae living in coral reefs die. This creates an area of dead, bleached coral reefs.

A healthy coral reef is one of the most biologically diverse and valuable ecosystems in the world. Algae living within the reef are the source of its color. When the algae die, the coral appears white or bleached.

CHAPTER SIX

Studying Biodiversity

Scientists called **ecologists** study plant and animal species. They try to understand each living thing and how it interacts with its environment. Ecologists work all over the planet. You can find ecologists studying biodiversity in the rainforests of Costa Rica, in the Pacific Ocean, and in the world's largest cities. Some ecologists study individual plants and animals. Others study an entire species. Still others study many species in an ecosystem.

Knowing what species live in an area helps ecologists decide how to protect habitats. Studying how living things behave helps ecologists understand ways they can protect biodiversity in the area.

whale shark

Sometimes ecologists work outside doing research on land or under water. They may set up an experiment to understand why a plant or animal is doing well or poorly in different habitats. They spend a lot of time identifying and **classifying** plants and animals. They measure how big they are. They observe the animal or plant to see what it eats, how it behaves, and where it lives. To help them observe the organism, an ecologist may take photos or video of species in their habitat.

Carl Linnaeus was a scientist who lived in the 1700s. He developed a system of classifying living things. Linnaeus divided the natural world into kingdoms. Then he split each kingdom into smaller and smaller groups. The living things in each group had similar characteristics. Today, scientists still classify living things using Linnaeus's groups: kingdom, phylum, class, order, family, genus, and species.

Carl Linnaeus

Tagging is one way ecologists learn about how an animal moves and behaves. The ecologist catches the animal in the wild and attaches an electronic monitor to it. The monitor tracks the animal's movements and sends the information to computers.

Leatherback turtle with electronic monitor

NORTH AMERICA

Galapagos Islands

SOUTH AMERICA

green sea turtle

Other times, ecologists study an entire ecosystem. They study a habitat to find and identify all the organisms that live there. Ecologists also take measurements about the habitat. They may measure temperature or the amount of nutrients in the soil or water.

The large elephant beetle lives in the rainforests of Costa Rica. Because of the destruction of rainforest habitat, the elephant beetles' mating grounds are extremely threatened.

Did You Know?

In Costa Rica, ecologists are working to identify all species that live in the country. They have identified nearly 3 million insects.

NORTH AMERICA

Costa Rica

SOUTH AMERICA

After working in the field, ecologists may return to the lab to study the information and samples they have collected. They study samples under a microscope and with other lab equipment. They look for patterns in DNA to identify and classify new organisms.

Ecologists studying mud worms may take mud samples from the bottom of a lake. They study the samples under a microscope to identify the worms that live in the mud and their behavior.

Ecologists may create computer models with their field data. With these models, they can predict how an animal or plant will behave in the future. With this information, ecologists can develop plans to manage habitats and protect biodiversity.

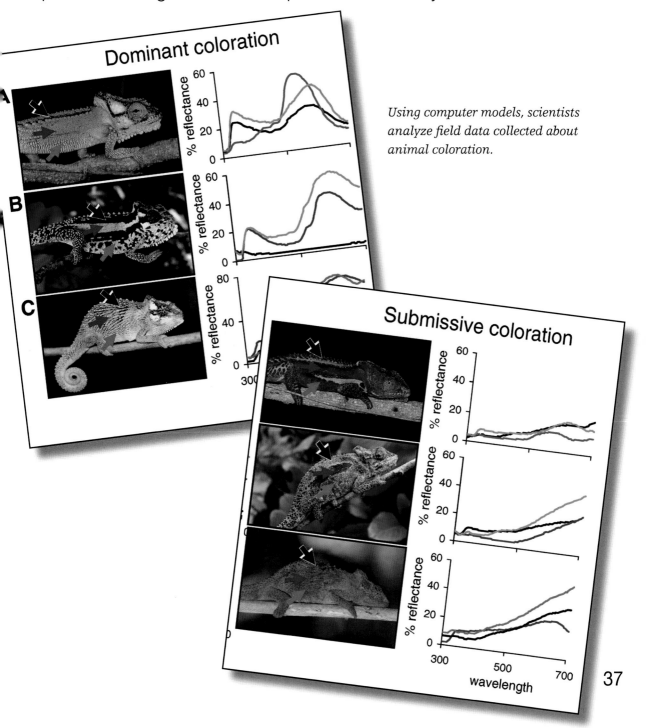

Using computer models, scientists analyze field data collected about animal coloration.

CHAPTER SEVEN

Protecting Biodiversity

All around the world, people are working to protect Earth's biodiversity. Two important ways to protect biodiversity are **conservation** and **preservation**.

Conservation is using natural resources responsibly. Conservation works to make sure that we don't run out of natural resources or cause a species to become extinct. Some conservation projects replace natural resources. Community groups may plant new, native trees.

Planting new native trees provides a valuable habitat for butterflies, birds, and other woodland wildlife.

Captive-breeding programs at zoos identify endangered species. They raise species in zoos and then release them into safe habitats in the wild. This is another critical step in the conservation process.

A U.S. Fish & Wildlife Service worker handles red wolf pups. Workers will care for the pups until they are old enough to be released into a safe habitat in the wild.

Preservation sets aside habitats as a home for plants and animals. It limits the use of these areas or organisms by people. Protected areas must be large enough to provide for the needs of the animals and plants that live there. Around the world, thousands of wilderness areas have been set up to protect plants, animals, and ecosystems.

NORTH AMERICA

Montana

SOUTH AMERICA

mountain goats

moose

grizzly bears

In Montana, Glacier National Park protects biodiversity by restricting mining and drilling activities.

Protecting biodiversity is not easy. Experts are constantly working to balance protecting Earth's natural resources with the needs of people who depend on those resources. Preservation is not an easy or quick task. It requires cooperation among many businesses, governments, and private landoweners.

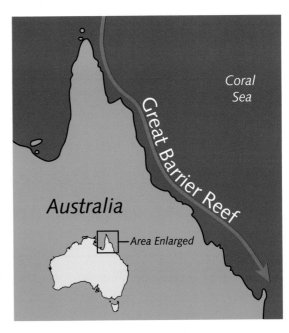

dugong

clownfish

great white shark

In Australia, no-fishing zones protect marine life around the Great Barrier Reef.

41

Hot Spots

To preserve biodiversity, scientists have named 34 biodiversity **hot spots** around the world. About 50 percent of the world's plants and 42 percent of vertebrate animals live in these hot spots. To be named a hot spot, the area must have at least 1,500 species of plants found nowhere else on Earth. It must also have lost at least 70 percent of its original habitat.

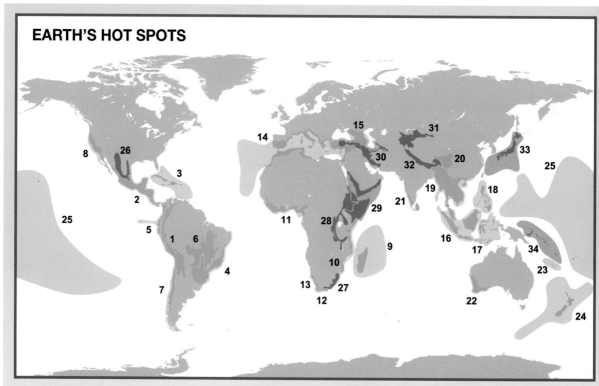

EARTH'S HOT SPOTS

1. The Tropical Andes
2. Mesoamerica
3. The Caribbean Islands
4. The Atlantic Forest
5. Tumbes-Chocó-Magdalena
6. The Cerrado
7. Chile - Valdivian Forests
8. The California Floristic Province
9. Madagascar and Islands
10. Coastal Forests of Eastern Africa
11. Guinean Forests of West Africa
12. The Cape Floristic Region
13. The Succulent Karoo
14. The Mediterranean Basin
15. The Caucasus
16. Sundaland
17. Wallacea
18. The Philippines
19. Indo-Burma
20. Mountains of Southwest China
21. Western Ghats and Sri Lanka
22. Southwest Australia
23. New Caledonia
24. New Zealand
25. Polynesia and Micronesia
26. The Madrean Pine-Oak Woodlands
27. Maputaland-Pondoland-Albany
28. The Eastern Afromontane
29. The Horn of Africa
30. The Irano-Anatolian
31. The Mountains of Central Asia
32. Eastern Himalaya
33. Japan
34. East Melanesian Islands

Scientists say that the world's biodiversity hot spots are shrinking. In the past, the 34 hot spots covered almost 16 percent of the Earth's land. Today, the hot spots only cover about 2.3 percent of the Earth's land. Protecting hot spots, by making them reserves or parks, could save many species from extinction. But, protecting hot spots is a worldwide effort. Each country is responsible for the biodiversity in their land. Scientists say that protecting the planet's species will need cooperation from everyone around the world.

State parks, like Big Basin Redwoods State Park in California, preserve and protect some of the richest hotspots of biodiversity around the world.

How You Can Help

Protecting biodiversity is important for everyone. If each person makes an effort to protect biodiversity, little things can add up to a big change. One of the most important ways to help biodiversity is to protect habitats. Explore the local habitats in your area. You can visit nearby national parks or nature reserves. Park rangers and naturalists can tell you about threatened species that live in the habitat and what is being done to protect them. You may want to volunteer to help clean up local beaches, parks, and fields where animals and plants live.

Not disturbing wildlife habitats is a simple way to protect biodiversity.

FIELD HABITAT PROJECT

This area has been set aside to provide habitat for ground-nesting birds and native wildflowers

PLEASE STAY ON TRAILS

A.C. SIGN SHOP

KEEP
Environmentaly Sensitive Habitat Area
OUT

You can also help biodiversity by reducing, reusing, and recycling what you can. Turning off lights saves energy. Reusing items saves on the resources needed to make new ones. Recycling also saves water, electricity, and energy. Making an effort to save energy and resources leaves more resources on Earth.

Packing your lunch in reusable containers is one way to reduce your consumption of energy and resources.

WHAT CAN YOU DO?

1. Control pet cats and dogs so they do not disturb wildlife.
2. Remove introduced weeds from your garden.
3. Eat new, biodiverse foods such as unusual fruits or vegetables.
4. Make wildlife welcome by building a place for shelter, food, and water in your backyard.
5. Volunteer your time with an environmental organization in your community.
6. Watch wildlife in their habitat, but leave them alone.

There are many other ways you can help preserve biodiversity. Working together, we can preserve and protect biodiversity around the world. That will mean a better future for all living things on Earth.

Glossary

adapted (uh-DAPT-ed): changed so that a living thing can fit better in its environment

biodiversity (bye-oh-duh-VURS-it-ee): when a wide variety of species live in a single area

biomes (BYE-ohmz): specific areas on Earth that have a similar climate

camouflage (KAM-uh-flahzh): to disguise something so that it blends in with its surroundings

classify (KLASS-uh-fye): to put things into groups according to their characteristics

climate (KLYE-mit): the usual weather in a place

conservation (kon-sur-VAY-shuhn): the protection of wildlife and natural resources

ecologists (ih-KOL-uh-jists): people who study plant and animal species and their environment

ecosystem (EE-koh-siss-tuhms): communities of living things and their physical environments

extinct (ek-STINGKT): when a living thing dies out

habitat (HAB-uh-tat): the place where a plant or animal lives

hot spots (HOT spots): places where biodiversity is threatened

introduced species (in-truh-DOOSS-ed SPEE-sheez): plants and animals brought from their natural habitat to live in a new habitat

microorganisms (mye-kroh-OR-guh-niz-uhmz): a living things that are too small to be seen without a microscope

organisms (OR-guh-niz-uhmz): living plants or animals

overconsumption (OH-vur- kuhn-SUHMP-shuhn): when people use natural resources faster than they can be replaced naturally

preservation (prez-ur-VAY-shuhn): protection of plants and animals by setting aside and protecting natural habitats

species (SPEE-sheez): one of the groups into which animals and plants are divided according to their shared characteristics

Index

adaptations   12-15

biodiversity   5-9

biome   10-12, 16

camouflage   14

climate change   24, 31

conservation   38, 39

ecologist   32-37

ecosystem   4, 8-10, 18, 21, 28, 31, 32, 35, 40

extinction   24, 30, 43

genes   7, 9

habitat loss   24, 25

hot spot   42, 43

introduced species   24, 26, 27

medicine   21-23

overconsumption   28

pollution   20, 24, 30

preservation   38, 40, 41

tagging   34

web of life   16

Websites to Visit

www.animal.discovery.com/guides/endangered/endangered.html

www.biodiversityhotspots.org

www.iucnredlist.org

About the Author

Carla Mooney has always been fascinated by animals, plants, and habitats big and small. She has a bachelor of science degree from the University of Pennsylvania and has written more than 25 books for young people. Today, she enjoys exploring local nature preserves with her husband and three children near Pittsburgh, Pennsylvania.

Ask The Author!
www.rem4students.com